voiceJunction

SATBarB unaccompanied

OXFORD

# Ben Parry

## Golden Slumbers

Difficulty level ● ● ◐ ○

*Dla Chóru Filharmonii Wrocławskiej i Agnieszki Franków-Żelazny*

# Golden Slumbers

Thomas Dekker (1572–1632),
Henry Chettle (1564–1606), and
William Haughton (d. 1605), adap.

Traditional
arr. **BEN PARRY**

Duration: 4 mins

Printed in Great Britain

OXFORD UNIVERSITY PRESS, MUSIC DEPARTMENT, GREAT CLARENDON STREET, OXFORD OX2 6DP

Golden slumbers kiss your eyes, Smiles awake you when you rise.

oo oo

oo oo

oo oo oo oo

oo oo

Sleep, pretty darling, do not cry, and I will sing a lullaby.

Do not cry, lullaby.

Do not cry, lullaby.

Do not cry, lullaby.

Do not cry, lullaby.

Lul - la - by, lul - la - by, lul - la - by, lul - la - by.

Lul - la - by,_____ lul - la - by.

Lul - la - by,_____ lul - la - by.

Lul - la - by,_____ lul - la - by.

Care_ you know not, there - fore sleep, While_ I o'er you watch do

Care_ you know not, there - fore sleep, While_ I o'er you watch.

Care_ you know not, there - fore sleep, While_ I o'er you watch do keep.

Care_ you know not, there - fore sleep, While_ I o'er you watch do keep.

Care you know not, there - fore sleep, While I o'er you watch do keep.

# voiceJunction

Voice Junction is an inspirational series of secular songs for all modern mixed-voice singing groups. A meeting point of various styles, the series is fresh, popular, and alternative in feel, and includes new original works—both accompanied and *a cappella*—alongside unique arrangements of well-known tunes. Whether performed by a one-per-part vocal group or a community choir, this is music that brings people together.

Photo: Susan Porter Thomas

Ben Parry studied at Cambridge University, singing in King's College Choir. He has toured as a member of The Swingle Singers, writing many of their arrangements and co-producing four albums. Parry is Artistic Director and Principal Conductor of the National Youth Choirs of Great Britain, Assistant Director of Music at King's College, Cambridge, and Director of London Voices. He has been commissioned by the BBC Singers, and his music has been heard at the BBC Proms. He is also a house composer for a commercial library music company and is credited on over 100 recordings.

**OXFORD**
UNIVERSITY PRESS

www.oup.com

ISBN 978-0-19-356031-4

9 780193 560314